# Treat Your Customers

HYPERION

*New York*

# Treat Your Customers

*Thirty Lessons*

*on Service and Sales*

*That I Learned at My Family's*

*DAIRY QUEEN® Store*

Bob Miglani

Library of Congress Cataloging-in-Publication Data
ISBN 1-4013-0198-3

Hyperion books are available for special promotions and
premiums. For details contact Michael Rentas,
Assistant Director, Inventory Operations, Hyperion,
77 West 66th Street, 12th floor, New York, New York 10023,
or call 212-456-0133.

FIRST EDITION

10   9   8   7   6   5   4   3   2   1

To my family, especially Mom,
who taught me the real value
of customer service

# Contents

# Contents

# Introduction

**W**hen I was growing up, I spent every summer working at my family's Dairy Queen store. At the time, it was mostly just a fun summer job. Now, looking back, I realize that those summers I spent behind the counter at our Dairy Queen were laying a foundation for my future as a businessman in the corporate world. Mastering the techniques my family used to serve and sell ice cream provided me with indispensable knowledge on the value of exceptional customer service. And I picked up more than a few techniques that have served me well as a Fortune 500 executive.

I didn't make the connection between selling ice cream and the corporate world until a few years ago when my two younger sisters and I were trying to talk my parents into selling the family ice cream business and retiring. My parents wouldn't have it. They love working and saw no need to sell the business when they were having such a good time. It was something that my mom said that made me reflect on my own career in a large company. She said, "Why should we sell the family business when it's given us so much happiness? I love seeing my customers smile every single day. Just look at what it has taught the three of you over all these years." After thinking about this for a few days I realized that I had learned a great deal growing up in the family business—much more than I could have ever anticipated. More importantly, I came to the realization that much of what I know about business and had been applying in my job at the big corporation, I had learned working at my family Dairy Queen store.

This book details the lessons that I learned from

my twenty-one years managing the Dairy Queen store which I have applied to my position in a Fortune 500 company for the last thirteen years. The business lessons in this book can provide you with clarity and perspective on some of the essential elements of running a successful business.

Sure, big business is complex and each company has its own unique traits, but having actually worked in both big business and small business, I've learned that there are a lot of similarities, especially when it comes to managing customers and employees. When you really think about it, many issues boil down to a few fundamental and simple truths.

I have had many roles within corporate America—from sales rep to public affairs director—and the lessons I learned from our DQ store were universally translatable. Whether I had to deal with customers, suppliers, employees, peers, or my managers, invariably something from the DQ experience came in handy. Some of these lessons helped me succeed during my years in sales and also during a difficult time in corporate headquarters when I had to build strong internal networks and virtual teams despite my distinct lack of authority and a nonexistent budget. I treated my peers and colleagues on these virtual teams just as I would my customers at the Dairy Queen store. Creating this kind of relationship proved invaluable later on. But the most important insight I obtained from the DQ experience was how to center an entire organization (a team, department, or division) around satisfying the customer.

### It's not just ice cream—it's Dairy Queen!

The Dairy Queen soft serve frozen dessert product was invented in 1938 in Green River, Illinois, by a father and son who had been experimenting with a new way of making a soft frozen dairy product for their dairy business. Using their friend's store as a test market, they ended up selling more than 1,600 servings of their first trial of soft serve within two hours. Thus Dairy Queen's soft serve frozen dessert product and its unique way of franchising stores was born—and it caught on quickly. Over the next few decades Dairy Queen's famous barn-shaped stores started popping up all over the Midwest. From 100 stores in 1947 it grew to 2,600 in 1955. (Today there are over 5,900 Dairy Queen restaurants in the United States, Canada, and twenty other countries.) During those early years and into the '70s and '80s, Dairy Queen did more than just serve great products—it became a household name. It became a place to take the family on a Sunday afternoon, a place where Little League teams celebrated after a ball game, and a place where customers were treated like a neighbor, a friend, or a family member.

In the late '80s, Dairy Queen continued to launch new products, including its famous "Blizzard" Flavor Treat which sold 175 million units in its first year of launch. In the '90s, it caught the eye of a famous customer who frequented his local DQ store in Omaha, Nebraska—Warren Buffett. He liked Dairy Queen so much that he bought the entire company in 1998. He was once quoted as saying, "It's a great business with great products and great people." Buffett's purchase was more than just a financial transaction. It represented the recognition of something more important—the strength of a business being run by people who believed in treating the customer right.

Today the Dairy Queen system of restaurants is one of the largest in the world. Many of the traditional barn-shaped "soft serve only" stores that we can remember visiting while growing up have been transformed into full-fledged restaurants that serve hot food as well as the famous frozen dessert products. But throughout the years one thing has remained constant: the commitment of each Dairy Queen store to exceptional service.

Many Dairy Queen store owners are families like mine who employ anywhere from five to fifty people and on a typical summer day may serve as many as seven hundred customers. Like many young teens, my first job was at the local Dairy Queen store in our small hometown in New Jersey. A couple of years later, my family bought our own DQ franchise where my sisters and I worked from high school through college.

Our family didn't just work at the Dairy Queen—we lived there. During the summer, all of us put in ten- to twelve-hour days, sometimes without a break for weeks. Over the dinner table we talked about nothing but the customers or the employees. Who needed more training, who was really good with customers, or which customers were beginning to become "regulars." Our conversations were always about the store and how we could make it better for the customer.

That focused attitude and the experiences in this book are what I carried with me as I moved up the ladder in the Fortune 500 company. Look at these lessons as if you were trying a number of different flavors of ice cream—some you might like and some you might not. But through it all, you might just find the one that you really like and it stays with you forever. And one day without even thinking about it, you apply a lesson or two and it helps bring great results to your business. So go ahead and take a bite. I'm sure you'll like it. Enjoy!

# 1

# They're Not Just Customers—They're People

**S**ummertime is understandably Dairy Queen's busiest season. And while serving ice cream doesn't sound like too stressful a job, waiting on long lines in the sweltering heat can get to the best of us. One particularly hot day, our employee Mike was serving a man who looked like he was in his midthirties. The air conditioner was on high, but with all the serving windows open, the heat was seeping in. A car alarm went off in the parking lot and the noise continued for about ten minutes. As Mike was putting some of the sundae cups into the customer's bag he said, "What's up with that guy—doesn't he know how to turn off his alarm?" The customer gave him a dirty look. "That's my father and he's having a little trouble with the car," he said. Mike's face drained completely of color. It was obvious Mike felt terrible about making that comment. It could have been anybody's father out there trying to turn off the car alarm.

Too often we forget that the people coming into our store or business are more than just consumers who drive our revenues. They are people with feelings, hopes, and problems just like the rest of us. The same things that upset us probably upset them too. By labeling anyone who walks into our store simply a client, a consumer, we are masking reality.

At our Dairy Queen business, we try very hard to treat the people who walk into our stores as neighbors, friends, and most importantly as human beings. If we do this and do it right, it results in our giving them the best service possible, effortlessly. It doesn't feel like a chore.

Case in point: One afternoon a woman walked up to the serving window accompanied by her three children, all of whom were under four years old. This mom seemed to have her hands full with her infant, car keys, purse, and the two cups and a cone she had just ordered. There were two other customers in line behind her and she was having trouble juggling all her things while trying to get her wallet out of her purse. I could have just waited for the money, said thanks, and moved on to the next customer waiting in line. But I didn't. I noticed she needed help so I offered her the chance to go get her kids settled on the benches outside and then, when she was ready, to come back and pay for the ice cream.

When she did come back to pay, I gave her extra napkins as well as some wet wipes because I knew that kids tended to make a mess. She was thankful for my help and relieved that her kids were happily eating away.

This customer was treated the way I would treat my friend or neighbor—with respect and consideration. I didn't look at her as a "consumer" who was taking up too much of my valuable time. And maybe she would no longer think of our store as just a retail establishment, but a place offering her something that could make her kids happy without a hassle.

By removing some of the words like "client" or "consumer" we remove the wall between "them" and "us." Without a wall to separate us, we are more able to treat them like real people. This results in their liking us even more, and hopefully becoming loyal customers.

Treat them well. It's not only good manners, it's good for business.

## 2

# Know Their Names and Their Favorite Flavor

In some industries, customers who frequent the business are known as "big fish," "heavy hitters," or "whales." In our Dairy Queen, they are simply called "regulars." These regulars are important because their purchasing habits make up a large percentage of our business. Over the years, my mom has gotten to know many of our regulars. She knows their names, where they work, the ages of their kids, and their favorite flavor of ice cream. "Karen likes to get three large lemon-lime Mr. Misty drinks, while Steve and his family prefer chocolate milk shakes every Sunday," she says to me. Each weekend or holiday I cover for her, there are always a few customers who ask about her—"Where's your mom? She's always so nice. She knows how to make my treat better than anyone." These are just a few of the sweet comments that Mom gets.

My mom's attention to return customers has a direct effect on sales. For example, a woman in her midsixties came into our store one day and ordered a small hot fudge sundae with mint chocolate chip ice cream. Over the course of three to four months, she would come in on Sunday afternoons every few weeks. During this time, my mom got to know what she liked. One day, my mom saw the woman get out of her car and had her sundae ready for her before she even had a chance to order it. After that day, this lady began coming in once a week. Over time, my mom not only got to know her name, but those of her grandkids and their friends as well. Next thing we knew, the lady's grandkids were part of a soccer team that liked to celebrate when they won a game. And guess where they came? Our Dairy Queen, of course.

This lady probably felt pretty good that day she went up to the serving window and found her order already made and ready to go. She probably appreciated that my mom cared enough to pay attention to what she liked. I don't think this lady would have become a regular customer if my mom didn't take the initiative to remember and prepare her ice cream before she even ordered it. And in our business, my mom isn't the only one with a good memory. All our employees are encouraged to put their "good memory" to use in a way that makes our customers feel valued.

What's the big deal about knowing the names and buying habits of customers? I believe that these customers become regulars partly *because* you know their names and buying habits. Sure, they might be regulars because they like your product or your convenient location. But by remembering their faces and what they like, you get a little closer to them, making them more comfortable with you and your business. By taking the time to get to know your customers and treat them like human beings, you build a bond. This bond is rewarded with customer loyalty and more frequent purchases.

Regulars are crucial to any business. You just don't wake up one day and have regulars walk into your place of business. It takes time, careful observation, and effort to build relationships with customers, some of whom actually end up becoming your regulars. Once you have cultivated this loyal customer base, get to know them even better and build programs and activities that suit their specific needs to keep them happy. Remember, it is these regulars that will generate the bulk of your revenues. And it all starts with simply remembering their name.

# 3

# The Customer
# Is Still Royalty

**A**sk anyone who has worked in customer service for a few years and he will tell you how much of a challenge it can be. He will tell you that customers don't know what they want, expect too much, want to pay almost nothing—and even when you give in to their demands, they still end up complaining about everything else. Serving customers each and every day is a tough job that requires a positive attitude and thick skin. And after some years in customer service, the physical and mental drain can make a person bitter, angry, or just unhappy. This results in a cynical and negative attitude toward the customer as well as co-workers. What's most dangerous is the thinking that the customer just doesn't matter—that no matter how poorly you treat the customer, he will continue to come into the store because the product or service is still valued. That the customer is not the king. It's easy to fall into this trap without even realizing it.

Forgetting the importance of keeping the customer happy can lead to the loss of business, as happened to a man I knew named Jimmy. The owner of Jimmy's Ice Cream, a store that was located about a hundred yards from our DQ, Jimmy was an older guy whose business had been around almost two decades. I assumed he had done pretty well due to the lack of real competition in the area. We never considered Jimmy's Ice Cream competition because our customers told us some pretty negative things about his business. For example, we were told that he was always bitter and rude and didn't do a very good job of cleaning his store. During our first couple of months in business, my dad went to "check him out" and came back with some interesting findings. The two customers who were in line at Jimmy's while my dad was there were treated poorly. One of the customers had asked for an empty cup for his young daughter, whose ice cream cone was dripping everywhere. Jimmy charged him twenty-five cents for the extra cup, much to the surprise of the customer. The second customer had mistakenly ordered a chocolate ice cream sundae when she really wanted vanilla. When she told Jimmy that she had made a mistake, he told her, "Well, that's not my fault—I'm sorry but I already made your sundae." The lady was nice enough not to argue.

It is relatively easy to see that Jimmy should've just given the cup for free to the first customer and made another sundae with vanilla ice cream for the second customer. It would have cost him a little bit more money, but it would be a small price to pay for customer satisfaction. He didn't do the right thing and instead his two customers left with bad tastes in their mouths.

Obviously, Jimmy didn't care how he treated his customers. Maybe being in business for so long had made him lazy. Or perhaps he thought because some customers were a nuisance, he could treat all of them any which way he wanted to—which was poorly. He thought wrong. Jimmy went out of business about a year and a half after we bought our store.

Even though we make it a point at our DQ to treat our customers fairly, I found myself falling into the "Jimmy trap" a couple of years ago. After a long and strenuous week at my corporate job, I was called upon to help out at the store during a hot summer weekend (funny how it's always a hot summer weekend when I'm working). Anyway, the hot and humid weather made some customers uncomfortable. They didn't like waiting a minute or two for their ice cream. Many were very rude and just didn't care how they treated me or the other employees. And so, unconsciously, I began to mimic their behavior and treat everyone with a bad attitude, even customers who were nice to me. One bad experience with a nasty customer can make you angry and ruin your mood for the entire day. That particular day, I soon found myself not smiling and although I wasn't that rude, I wasn't treating customers well. It wasn't until we closed the store that night that one of the employees asked me what was wrong. That question woke me out of my negative trance. Sometimes you just don't realize your behavior until someone points it out.

As difficult as it is to manage tough customers, never forget that these very people are the reason you have a business. Customers are fickle, difficult, and a real pain in the neck at times. But the bottom line is that without them, you won't make any money. Getting paid to provide a value to someone who needs your product or service—regardless of his temperament—is what business is all about. Customers may at times be difficult to serve but don't let anyone tell you that customers are not important. They still are—and always will be—and you've got to treat them like they're royalty if you want to have a successful business.

# 4

# Don't Make
# Them Wait

Today's business environment is fast-paced. Whether you're in New York, Dallas, or Little Rock, these days everyone is in a hurry. The typical customer expects goods and services to be provided equally fast. From family obligations like picking up the kids after practice to the demands of a hectic career, people have too much to do. As service providers we have to respect that—and get them what they want as quickly as possible.

The first thing we teach each of our employees is that they should be constantly aware of a new customer walking into the store. The second is that no customer should have to wait to be served.

Too often when you go to a coffee shop or a clothing retailer in the mall, you see lots of people working but only one or two people at the checkout counter waiting on the long line of customers. The store's managers are basically allowing customers who are ready to give them money to wait in long lines. I don't get it. It's annoying, frustrating, and most of the time, will leave the customer with a negative feeling toward the business. Customers will begin to associate your establishment with slow service.

It's the same thing in the food service business. What we always try to avoid are frustrated customers. Customers who know what they want and are standing in line are served as quickly as possible by our employees. Sure there can be lines at our DQ during the summer even with all our employees serving customers. And sometimes we're even short-staffed. But most of the time, we serve our customers promptly so they don't have to wait.

An example of a business that has quality products, but not quality service, is one my wife and I used to frequent. One of our favorite Friday-night rituals is going out for pizza and ice cream. Living in New York City, we have many restaurant choices, but prefer this small pizza place in lower Manhattan and an equally small ice cream shop near a university neighborhood. The people working at the ice cream shop are in their early twenties and blend nicely with the local coeds. The ice cream is great but the servers talk a whole lot among themselves while they're serving customers. One night, as a young lady was scooping up my ice cream, she was in the middle of a conversation with her co-worker, who was doing nothing. It took her longer to fill up my ice cream cup because she was busy talking instead of focusing on serving me. After having a similar negative experience a few times, we just stopped going. Even though the ice cream is delicious, it's not worth the time it takes to get it. Any customer who is made to wait an unreasonable amount of time before being served often comes to the same conclusion.

The primary job of a business is to sell something to its customers. Everything else—the cleaning, the organizing, the stocking, etc.—is also important but not the real reason you open your business. You open the door each day to serve the people who come into your store. So do just that. Every employee should be capable, trained, and ready to serve customers from the first day on the job. Sure, they're in training and need to be shown how to do it right and that's perfectly fine. But don't have five employees in the store and only two serving customers with a long line—have them all manning the cash registers to get the customers on their way.

Customers need to feel that the business is attentive to their needs. Long lines often indicate uncaring employees and will create a negative impression of your business. Create an environment that is purely focused on the customer. Acknowledge them when they're walking into the store. Observe and listen to their needs. Having attentive and enthusiastic employees helps to ensure that your customers don't wait. And get rid of needless distractions and focus your employees on their only job—serving those customers. Doing this will make a lasting, positive impression on your customer.

**5**

# Once in a While, Taste Your Own Ice Cream

**B**efore my family bought our own Dairy Queen store, I spent a summer working at a neighboring Dairy Queen owned by a Hungarian family. Barbara, the tall blond fifty-year-old owner, was teaching me how to make the strawberry topping. There really wasn't much to it—you open up the big red container of premade strawberry topping and add a touch of strawberry flavoring to give it a sweeter taste and a richer color. When she asked me to get a spoon so that she could try it herself I didn't know what to think. She said it needed a little more flavoring so I added it. Upon seeing my slightly puzzled expression, she explained that she liked to taste everything she made and, once in a while, even the things she didn't make in the store, like the hard ice cream or the milk shake. This ensured that the customers got fresh and great-tasting products every time. Her philosophy was that if it wasn't good enough for the owner, then it wasn't good enough for the customer.

I never forgot Barbara's lesson. In the early years of our own Dairy Queen business, we were so paranoid that we would test almost everything all the time. This proved difficult to keep up given the vast number of products we sold (not to mention the inevitable impact on our waistline!). Our policy now is to randomly spot-check all of our products to ensure they are fresh and tasty.

I learned to recognize the value of the random spot-check the hard way. I was helping out at the store one Saturday after Halloween some years ago. The weather had been unseasonably cold all week but the weekend was really warm. I went straight to the store without eating breakfast. As soon as I got there, I felt a little hungry and made myself a banana milk shake. After a few gulps, I realized that it didn't taste good. I checked the expiration date and apparently the milk was beginning to go bad. Normally, we have such high turnover that our products are always fresh, but on occasion ice cream can go bad—it is of course made from milk. I'm glad that I drank that shake instead of one of our customers.

Once in a while, you've got to taste your ice cream—whether you make it yourself or not. Whether you sell food, clothing, pots and pans, cars, toothbrushes, or services, you've got to sample your own products to make sure they live up to the promise that you're making to customers.

And it's not just about the products we serve at the store. It is also about the outward appearance of our store and the customer service provided by our employees. I'm a bit picky, and for me, in order to truly understand what our customers see, I have to go outside the store, check out the menu, and get served by one of our employees. Sure people can tell me what the experience is like, but until I see it and experience it for myself, I'm not satisfied.

I can't imagine running a business, whether it's a Dairy Queen or a major Fortune 500 company, without having a real *feel* for customers. How can you run a business without talking to a customer every now and then? On a recent television interview on CBS, I saw the CEO of a major Fortune 500 company talking about the day she had spent working alongside one of her employees on the front line serving customers at their retail outlet. It was part of a CBS series called *Changing Places,* which required CEOs to work in the trenches with their employees in hands-on areas of the business like manufacturing, an assembly line, or in a retail store. She said although the work was hard, she found it to be very rewarding because it gave her a good idea of how the company's operations really work. Based on her one day in the retail store, she planned to make some specific changes to her company's policies.

It's a good business practice to go on the front lines occasionally. It not only helps to get a flavor for the business, but also gives the employees a sense that there's someone in the corporate office who actually cares. Knowing the leadership of the company is in touch with the realities of the business also builds employee confidence.

If you want to know how your business is being perceived, get out of your office and check out your business from the outside. Take a day and get out in the field with a salesperson or someone in the assembly line. Do it often enough so that you don't lose sight of what's real. Otherwise, you might end up selling sour milk shakes.

# 6

# If They Ask for a Medium Cone—Give Them a Medium Cone

When making a soft serve ice cream cone in our Dairy Queen store, we don't simply measure the serving size by the height of the ice cream. Rather, we place it on a small scale to see if it's the right weight in addition to giving it a look-over to ensure it's the right size. To make certain we remain consistent, we work very hard in training our employees to weigh each cone for a short period of time before they are ready to just use their eye. A few weeks and a few hundred cone orders later, a server gets used to making a small, medium, or large cone at the right weight without having to weigh it on the scale. It's not a perfect science but it's as precise as we can get with this kind of product.

One day, my mom was training a new employee, and the customer that she and the new trainee were serving ordered a medium vanilla cone. As usual, the trainee made the cone with Mom's help and served it. The cone weighed the right amount and also passed the "eye test." The next customer in line also asked for a medium vanilla cone. The trainee made this one herself with my mom observing from a distance. This time, the cone barely resembled the cone that had been served right before. It was a bit fatter on the bottom, shorter in height, and definitely weighed a lot more than the previous cone. Obviously the trainee was a bit nervous making the cone herself. The customer looked at his cone and looked back at the cone served to the previous customer, pausing briefly after recognizing that he didn't get the same product as the person before him. Nevertheless, he smiled, paid for the cone, and left.

Now, usually it's a bit difficult to "correct" the size of the cone without wasting the ice cream. Nevertheless, we try to make our product as identical as possible. In this case, it was not such a big deal, but it leads to an important point in managing customers on a daily basis. And that is the importance of CONSISTENCY.

Now imagine both of these customers are friends. In comparing their cones, the one who has the smaller cone thinks he's been cheated even though they both ordered the same thing. Or what if the same customers had come back to our DQ the next day and were served by another employee who made a medium-sized cone that was perfect in weight but did not look as big as the ones they got yesterday? They're not going to know that they got a perfect-sized cone today. They're simply going to think that they got cheated because the cone they got yesterday looked *bigger*.

This is the point: Customers don't know about business policies or procedures and don't really care how things are done behind the scenes. They just want the medium cone they ordered to look as close as possible to the one they got yesterday or the one the guy got in front of them. That's it. Whether you're operating a small business or a large one, you've got to satisfy customers on a daily basis. There are so many chances to screw it up and consistency in product or service is not one of those things that you want to screw up.

Customers expect to get what they ask for: no more, no less. That's why they come to you in the first place. Business gurus preach about doing things differently all the time and it *is* good to do things differently. But if you can't deliver your product or service with the same consistency, what good is novelty? Don't try to do something extraordinary that you can't deliver each and every time. There are countless bankrupt businesses founded on "novelty" customer service. Customers have certain expectations when they call you or walk into your place of business. Don't let them down by surprising them every time.

Strive to give your customers the same high-quality product or service every time. Being predictable in business is not a bad thing. Your customers will come into your place of business or request your product because they know that you're going to give them what they want with no surprises. Fundamentally, this is what we all want, isn't it? The same size medium cone as the next person. So the next time your customer orders one of your products, give them exactly what they ask for. Delivering high-quality, consistent product or service keeps your customers coming back for more.

# 7

# Don't Serve
# Rotten Bananas

Jessica had been working at our Dairy
Queen store for a few months. She had
proven herself to be a fast learner who lis-
tened closely to the needs of the customers
and served them quickly. One day one of our
regular customers came in and ordered a banana split. Jessica began making the banana
split when she noticed that the bananas on
the counter were a bit on the overripe side.
She asked me if these bananas were okay to
be served or if she should go in the back and

get fresh ones. I looked at the bananas and they looked fine to me. They weren't black and soft but a little on the overripe side nonetheless. I would have eaten them myself with no problem. Looking at the box in the back, I noticed we had an entire box full of similarly ripe bananas and realized that we had to sell the ones in the front, otherwise we would be throwing away the whole lot in a couple of days. I told Jessica to go ahead and use the bananas she had in her hand.

The customer she had served the overripe banana came back a few days later. While I was serving him, I asked him how he liked the banana split that he ordered the last time he was here. He said it was fine but I could tell from his tone that he was mostly being polite, and that he hadn't particularly liked the banana split. I casually and honestly told him that the reason I was asking was because "I think we might have given you an overripe banana and I just wanted to see if it was okay." Surprised that I remembered such a small detail, he opened up and told me that the banana was okay but the banana split didn't taste as good as it usually does. I thanked him for his opinion and assured him, half-jokingly, that in the future he would get only "perfect bananas."

Within the course of each day, a businessperson has to make split-second decisions while taking into account many factors, including the customer, business owner or manager, finances, employees, suppliers, and community. Sometimes it is the little details, like an overripe banana. Other times it's something bigger. I made the wrong call on that overripe banana, placing a greater weight on my desire not to have too much inventory of bad bananas when I should have just served this guy a fresh one.

You have to give your customers the very best product each and every time. They know a good product when they see or taste one. They're willing to part with their hard-earned cash to buy something of quality. So do the right thing and give it to them. Don't hesitate. Don't serve rotten bananas. If somehow you've made a mistake, own up to it and fix it to make that customer happy. Give him or her something free and apologize profusely. Your customers will appreciate it and your business will benefit.

# 8

# Never Forget
# the Plain Old Vanilla

In the early '90s, we started getting a lot of competition from new ice cream retailers like TCBY and Ben & Jerry's. Not only did they offer some innovative flavors of ice cream, but sold frozen yogurt as well, which was a new product that really took the market by storm. Flavors like chocolate chip cookie dough, fudge brownie, and screwy strawberry were big hits. Four out of every ten customers would ask for frozen yogurt or one of those wild flavors. And while Dairy

Queen restaurants were well established, having been around for over fifty years, we just hadn't kept up with the market as well as our smaller and much nimbler competition. We weren't as inventive with our flavors as our rapidly changing customer base wanted us to be. So, we brought in frozen yogurt and some hot new treats like the DQ Blizzard (which is a blend-in of soft serve ice cream and in-gredients like candy, or cookies). Although the Bliz-zard treat was a success, we were still not growing as fast as the new guys on the block.

My younger sister, being an impressionable young teenager in the '90s, would drive us crazy asking us to expand our variety of flavors to better reflect what she thought were the hot new trends. She begged me to try to convince our parents to stock up on all these wild new flavors. One day, I lis-tened. We ended up ordering many of the hot fla-vors that were popular with customers her age. They sold well for a few months but not as well as I had hoped. In fact, one summer weekend, we had so much inventory of these flavors that we simply forgot to order the supply of the plain old vanilla. And wouldn't you know it—vanilla was the most in-demand flavor that weekend. And we were out of it!

No matter how "hot" a new flavor might be, most people just want vanilla. Nobody talks about TCBY frozen yogurt anymore or about any of those crazy flavors. In fact, Dairy Queen has discontinued frozen yogurt from most of the stores in the United States due to a lack of consumer demand. Over the decades I've been in the DQ business, vanilla and chocolate have never been out of the Top 5 flavors served at Dairy Queen restaurants.

You should never lose sight of the product or service that is at the heart of your business. It is what your business is known for or what people associate with your brand. And what brings in most of your revenues. Sure, you've got to try new things based on trends and customer needs, but don't forget about your cash cow—that plain old vanilla.

## 9

# Always Replace
# a Dropped Cone

**W**e've all witnessed the following tragic situation: One Saturday afternoon, a mother brings her three young kids into our store and gets them all a cone. After paying for it, they go outside to the benches and as they are walking, one of the kids drops the cone. The child's smile turns to horror— or even worse, tears. The mom comes back and orders another cone. Just as one of our new employees is about to collect the money,

I stop her. Citing our "policy" that every child goes home happy, I give the cone to the mom for free. Grateful and pleasantly surprised, the happy mom thanks me and brings the fresh new ice cream cone to the eagerly waiting child. This situation happens about a half dozen times a month. We replace the dropped cone every time.

Even if we're out of stock on the flavor of ice cream the customer orders, we usually make up for it by not charging them for the hot fudge or whipped cream they might get on top of their replacement flavor. Why do we do this? Because it preserves the integrity of our business and it's the right thing to do.

Many other businesses do the same. I've seen a mail-order company that ships their goods at no cost if they don't have the product in stock at the time of a customer's order. Or a shoe company that replaces a pair of shoes free of charge if there's a defect in the shoe even after months of use.

It is better to sacrifice some short-term revenues for the long-term preservation of the integrity of the business. Replace a dropped cone or ship the item for free. Not only does it make the customer happy, it's the right thing to do.

# 10

# Want Whipped Cream and Nuts on That?

**M**ost customers who walk into our Dairy Queen are usually in a hurry. When serving them, our natural tendency is to give them exactly what they requested and then get them out of the store quickly. While this is difficult enough sometimes, it doesn't maximize the potential opportunity you may have for that individual customer. When we're training each employee, we focus on the piece of customer interaction that we commonly refer to as the "up-sell."

A DQ sundae is served in the standard Dairy Queen way: delicious soft serve ice cream with only one topping so as not to take away from the natural flavor of soft serve and fruit or fudge topping.

But that doesn't mean that each customer walks out of the store with their sundae made this way. A customer *can* choose to add or modify their product as they wish with whipped cream, nuts, sprinkles, or something else. In fact in our store, every customer is kindly asked if they "would like whipped cream and nuts on top." We try to offer this in a way that is appetizing and appealing to the senses, as if the whipped cream and nuts naturally belong there. Some customers politely decline, but most do in fact opt for that extra topping, giving us an added profit.

Making that extra fifty cents for each sundae is important because getting customers to come into your business is hard enough—so when they're in there, you want to maximize each dollar from the visit. It usually takes about one to two minutes to serve a customer in our business. By adding the up-sell to each customer, we spend only a few more seconds and end up adding about a 5 percent profit to the sale!

Consistently offer the up-sell to each customer. If a customer is already in your store, grab that opportunity to provide something a little extra that they may want. It's fine if they don't, but you never know unless you ask. Training employees to sell is very important. Selling is one of those traits that is the most valuable in any business or job but one of the hardest to do well. Getting it right can do wonders for your bottom line.

# 11

# The Cherry
# Is Always Free

So, how do we train our employees to "up-sell" consistently? Over years of selling for both Dairy Queen and a Fortune 500 company, I've learned that the key to successful selling is *natural conversation focused on the emotional feeling associated with the product or service*.

After putting whipped cream and nuts on top of a sundae, we top it off with a sweet, red cherry. But we don't charge them extra for this. For some reason, people feel good when you top off a sundae with a cherry. Maybe it sounds too corny but it's almost as if the sundae is not complete without the cherry on top.

Having served a few hundred thousand sundaes over the years, I've noticed that there seems to be this twinkle in the eyes of those who opt for the extra topping that says, "This is what a sundae is all about!" This is exactly the emotional feeling we want to create with the customer. It's not about the cherry on top per se but the sweet memories associated with the product. This kind of sensory reminder can really make a person's day.

Anyone can say, "Would you like whipped cream, nuts, and a cherry?" But soft and friendly language such as, "How about topping it off with some whipped cream, nuts, and a cherry?" provides a natural way to reach the customer. Or my personal favorite, "How about the works—whipped cream, nuts, and of course the cherry?" By incorporating our up-sell into natural conversation with the customer, we come pretty close to getting a "Yes" 90 percent of the time.

Use an emotional and natural way to engage the customer when selling. Have a conversation. It's less about the "cherry" and more about the emotional feeling that you attach to the product or service you are selling. In our business, it's a cherry that symbolizes a "complete" sundae. In other businesses it may simply be the way you approach a customer or deliver them the service. By talking with your customers naturally and associating the benefit of your product or service with a certain feeling, you have a higher chance of sales success. A fragrance company never tells you the ingredients in a fragrance—just that it will make you feel macho or beautiful. Successful car commercials often focus on a driver's experience navigating through beautiful beaches or forests during a sunset. Give your customers a cherry on top of their sundae and you'll not only make their day but also make your business successful.

# 12

## Greet Them and Leave Them With a Smile

Any day of the week, we see hundreds of customers come in and out of our store—some who are calm and in a good mood, while others are obviously rushed, and just fly in and out of the store quickly. The first thing many people think about when they walk into our store or any retail establishment is, "I hope this salesperson will pay attention to my needs and get me what I want without a hassle." Having this in mind, the first interaction with the customer is really important. We have to educate our employees to make the first contact as soon as the customer steps inside and to do it with a smile. Welcome them with warm, friendly, and conversational greetings such as, "Hi, how are you doing today?" or "How's it going today?" Both convey a personal touch.

While the traditional "Hi, may I help you?" is fine, a conversational greeting is natural and tends to put people at ease. It makes them feel like they are not just another customer. Across the United States, the "super-retailers" have institutionalized the formal greeting by appointing someone to greet customers as they enter the store. While this is an excellent way to introduce a human touch to a colossal store, it can become impersonal over time.

Greeting customers with a smile is important because it sets the tone for the rest of the experience. Whether it's on the phone or in person, a positive feeling crossing over to the customer is invaluable for making a customer happy. A smile is not as simple as it may appear because it can convey so many things—attentiveness, confidence, enthusiasm, openness, and a can-do attitude. By greeting your customers with a smile, you are saying to them, "You're going to have a nice experience here because I'm going do my best to get you what you want."

Make your first contact with your customer in a friendly, warm-and-fuzzy way. You want to make the customer feel at ease speaking with your employees. It shouldn't feel perfunctory, like simply part of the act of taking the order and delivering a product. A nice greeting sets a positive tone and offers a natural vehicle to show your customers the specialness of your place. By greeting your customers with a smile, you will be on your way to having customers who leave with a smile.

# 13

# The Boss Is Not
# the Customer

**F**or a sixteen-year-old, Jonathan was a tall kid. He came in for a job application with his mom, a cute little lady with a happy-go-lucky attitude. Probably because of his height, people expected him to be tough and loud-mouthed. As it turned out, Jonathan was quite shy and had a soft-spoken voice. As I started to work with him, I noticed he was seriously attentive to my words and followed direction precisely. Over the course of the next few weeks, he proved himself to be a well-behaved kid who followed our instructions to the very last detail. Jonathan always took heed to our business policies, never caused any problems, and never complained.

But after a couple of weeks on the job we started getting mixed comments on his service from a few of our regular customers. Upon exploring this further, we learned that Jonathan was doing all the things we asked him *only* when we were around. In front of us, he would greet customers appropriately, clean the counters, refill the machines, and help other employees. But when we weren't there, he wasn't living up to our expectations. Some of our regular customers who know firsthand how much we value good customer service were the ones who told us about Jonathan's bad behavior. They revealed that he would be in the back of the store when there were many customers waiting, deliberately take his time when making products, and leave things a mess when he could have cleaned up a bit. We confirmed this when we made a surprise visit to the store one evening and found him doing inappropriate things.

When we questioned Jonathan about it, all we got was an apologetic smile with no eye contact. After speaking to him about this, I realized that he just didn't appreciate right from wrong in this case. He thought the objective of the job was simply to make me and my sisters happy—and he had been doing that. He wasn't focused on the main purpose of his job—to make the customer happy.

Jonathan hadn't intended any harm, but no one makes money on good intentions. I had a talk with him that day that made him think about his job differently, which led to a change in his behavior. Simply put, I told him that his job was not to impress me, but to impress the customers. And you impress the customer by serving consistent, quality product with a positive attitude. If the customer is happy then I, as the owner, will be happy. It was the simplest element of business to explain but it required that straightforward communication.

Too often, we either forget to explain the vision for our employees or just don't remind them enough about who the real customer is. Some of them tend to think that just because the managers determine the raises, they're the ones you have to impress. Countless boardroom presentations have been developed solely for impressing the boss. But a good manager knows that kissing up doesn't sell product—it just wastes valuable time and resources. A good manager sees right through it.

Whatever the industry, employees must have clarity of purpose of their job. They must know who the real customer is or they will simply try to impress the boss. Whether it's customer satisfaction, high product quality, or efficient logistics, managers must provide clarity of purpose. Employees need to be shown the goalpost, to have a specific objective to work toward. They may not have that in their personal life but in a structured environment such as a business, this is something they expect.

At our store, the approach is simple—each customer must feel good about their experience through the delivery of a quality product and consistent service. Everything employees do must revolve around that simple expression of customer satisfaction—a smile. Unless you make that clear to your team members or employees, they will do what they perceive to be important. And like Jonathan, they may make the mistake of satisfying the boss before the customer. Without a customer, there is no business, no employee, and no boss. So, tell them clearly, tell them often, but certainly tell them that the boss is not the customer—the *customer* is the customer!

# 14

# Become a Cake Expert

In the early years of our Dairy Queen business, ice cream cakes were not a popular item in our store. Once our main competitors began massively advertising their ice cream cakes, we started to see more and more customers ask about specialty cakes. The traditional DQ cake is filled with the soft serve, a layer of fudge and crunch, and a few flowers on the top for decoration. That's it—very simple. But customers wanted pretty drawings of clowns, faces of their kids, and more. Some customers wanted cakes that had images of their children's favorite cartoon characters on them, while others requested the whole cake to be in the shape of a popular television character. This trend toward specialty cakes caught us by surprise and unfortunately we had to decline many of these customer requests because we didn't know how to make them. Although Dairy Queen restaurants offered prepackaged frozen cakes, we really didn't know how to satisfy this new market for the custom-made variety.

We needed to figure out how to manage this growing demand. We had denied these requests in the past because they were time-consuming, costly, and complicated. But as time went on, and the demand for these cakes just grew, we began seriously losing business to our competitors. So we decided to hire a cake consultant—someone who knew how to make the types of cakes our customers were willing to pay a premium for. She lasted about two weeks. Highly paid, she never showed up on time and threatened to leave the first week unless we paid her even more money. My mom didn't tolerate this brand of extortion and neither did I. But we still had a problem: How could we handle the cake demand?

One Saturday afternoon soon after, my older sister walked into our Dairy Queen store just as a customer was asking one of the employees if we offered ice cream cakes decorated with clowns and balloons. My sister responded, "Sure, we'll have it for you tomorrow." With a can-do attitude, my sister took a shot at making this specialty cake and did a great job. She had always been the type to experiment in the kitchen, baking all sorts of sweet things like pies, cookies, and more. She was a natural who wasn't formally trained in how to make specialty cakes, but gave it a shot anyway. After her first cake was such a success we agreed that she would become our cake expert, and we would send her to specialty classes in order to perfect this new expertise. And that's exactly what she did. After taking a series of cake decoration training sessions at a local department store, she was hot! She gained the confidence to try new things and sure enough, new customers came. Once customers found out that our store was making cakes with rich, robust colors and innovative pictures and shapes, our cake sales grew tremendously.

Learning and adapting to new trends and technologies is essential to success in the marketplace. Every now and then in any business, customers will want new and unique products or services. In our case, we didn't initially have the knowledge to satisfy the new customer demand for specialty ice cream cakes. So we took a shot at learning this new "technology" and experimented with ways to embrace it. We may have stumbled at first, but eventually we figured out a way to adopt this new product on our own terms—and found success.

Each and every day, technology introduces new ways to do the classical things or create new products. We must not only adapt to this new technology or trend but adopt it vigorously and integrate it into our normal business. Sure, we could have hired someone else to do this for us, and hiring a consultant may work in some cases, but we wanted to ensure that we kept this competitive advantage inside the store, and for us that meant training an existing employee. So, don't be afraid of new things. Change is always going to be around. It's what makes the business fun. It's what forces us to learn new things. Embrace it by educating yourself and your people. Otherwise, you'll still be selling the same old cakes.

# 15

# Don't Raise Prices
# if Mom Feels
# Guilty

**E**very spring when we reopen our store, one of the most difficult things we have to do is to recheck our prices and make sure they are in line with the realities of today's competitive marketplace. And so each spring, we reassess the pricing of almost our entire line of product and see where we must raise our prices and where we can keep them the same or lower them.

Pricing is a key driver of success in any business. But it is getting harder and harder to judge how best to handle pricing each year. Labor and supply costs are increasing dramatically and with new competition popping up all around, it is difficult to increase prices. We have to be very careful about balancing the need to raise prices with the desire to keep our customers from going somewhere else. When considering price changes, we consider four factors:

1. Competition. Our main competitor is quite a distance from our Dairy Queen store so we don't really bother thinking twice on this one. Even when we had the Häagen-Dazs and the Carvel down the road from us, we never felt that we had to price our products lower to get our customers into our store. Our customers come into our store because we offer good products, and good, clean, friendly service. This doesn't mean that we can price high—just fair. Bottom

line—unless you're selling a commodity, people are not as price sensitive as one might believe.

**2.** The rounding test. Customers typically don't remember prices unless you tell them about it through advertising or other promotions. If you ask the typical consumer how much a sundae costs, you'll get a wide range of answers, but most people will say around $3 when the real price may be $2.70. When the real price is $2.25, they'll probably say $2. Most people will never get it right on the nose—they simply just round up or down. And so when pricing our products, we typically round up if we believe that we can do this without turning off the customer. So for a product that is priced at $2.85, we might raise it to $2.90 or $2.95. For the customer, it's usually not a big deal because it's still "around three bucks." But for us it means either a 1.75 percent increase or a 3.5 percent one—which is quite significant to the bottom line.

3. Market research. Just because we're a DQ doesn't mean that we don't have sophisticated market research telling us a thing or two about our pricing. Occasionally, our regional marketing staff from DQ headquarters does some market research where they tell us about consumer trends, competitive pricing, and more. While this is important, usually this doesn't change our day-to-day procedures much because of the huge differences from one part of the state to another. We use it as a tool to gauge whether we are really off the mark or not, but that's about it.

4. Mom's Guilt Test. None of the other tests applies if our prices don't pass Mom's guilt test. She serves hundreds of customers each day, many of them three or four times a

week. Over time, she's gotten to know so many of them and has developed a sense of responsibility for them. The test is simple— if she feels that the price is too high for most of our customers—no increase. She knows how customers might react when making a purchase and wants to do the right thing by taking into account their feelings. Deep inside each one of us is a feeling—an instinct—that comes to the fore when we're making important decisions. This is simply that feeling taken to the level of decision making. You have to feel that you're not cheating your customers—that you're just being fair. That's all. You shouldn't feel ashamed of your prices. And if you are pricing too high, you would feel some guilt about it.

One year, I wanted to raise the price of one of our core Top 5 products by five cents. Mom would not let me do it. It would have meant a decent increase in our bottom-line profits but Mom's argument was that she wouldn't be able to look her customers in the eye if we made the price change. To compromise, we didn't increase the price for all Top 5 products, but did do it for a few.

It's not rocket science to price products fairly. Use some market-analytic tools, good judgment, common sense, and be fair about it. Don't cheat people, but don't be afraid to do the right thing for your bottom line either. Whatever you do, have your customers in mind. Be fair to them and your business will benefit.

# 16

# When It's Time to Lean, It's Time to Clean

Rainy days are typically slow in the ice cream shop business. We may have a couple of employees in the store who have busied themselves by filling up all the containers for toppings and flavors while waiting for customers to show up. The employees believe that everything is ready to go but since there are no customers coming they do what they feel is natural—nothing at all. As they are waiting around, they start to lean back on the counter and begin chatting to one another.

This behavior may seem natural and logical to some, but not to our family, and not in our store. At the store, my family is constantly moving because there's always something that needs to get done. When you have hundreds of different types of flavors, treats, cups, spoons, etc., there's always something that either needs filling or cleaning. And when you're constantly moving, time goes by quickly. We strongly encourage this policy of keeping busy with all of our employees through a phrase that we use now and then: "When it's time to lean, it's time to clean."

The idea behind this is to encourage our employees to be fully engaged in the business by finding new things to do during slow periods. We do this by getting them to perform tasks around the store—from cleaning the shelves or organizing the stockroom more efficiently, to making cakes, or simply practicing customer service issues. Often, we even get them to practice writing on a cake or making novelty treats. Whatever the tactic, the objective is to have productive employees. The best employees are the ones who always keep busy on their own by finding creative things to do that add value to the business. But sometimes they need encouragement—they are not sure what to do. And so we tell them directly through our "no leaning" policy.

Create a policy within your business that encourages action. Not simply for the sake of killing time but for getting your people prepared for when it does stop raining and a hundred people rush into your store. It's about encouraging your employees, colleagues, and team to keep moving forward. It's also about motivating them to get off their backs and take action on their own! My mom hates it when employees lounge around or just stand with their hands in their pockets. She pushes them to find things to do on their own because there is always a lot to do. You just have to be smart and look around and find it. In our experience some employees get a little lazy when they don't have any customers and eventually this lackadaisical attitude seeps into everything they do in the workplace. To discourage this type of behavior, we give them small projects to work on that will train them in a different area of the business. This training comes in handy later on. To get the best results from your employees, keep them engaged in unique projects to help them grow and develop into productive individuals. The objective is really to create an environment where employees stay motivated.

# 17

# Gotta Love Your
# Soft Serve

Over the summer, my sisters and I give up our weekends off from our regular jobs to do something some of my friends in the corporate world admit they could never do: work behind the counter at our parents' Dairy Queen store. Often I've been asked why we do it when we may not really need to, given that we have enough employees to cover. Sure, it's partially the guilty feeling we get knowing that if it's not us, it's our mom at the store on her feet all day selling ice cream. And another reason is that we're a little addicted. We're so accustomed to going each weekend that when we don't have to go in, we don't know what to do with our free time.

The more compelling reason is that we love the DQ business. We love it because it forces us to think differently, to be creative, to face new challenges all the time. We love the glorious smile it brings to the face of a little baby girl who has tasted the soft serve vanilla for the very first time. Or how it brings families closer—gets them out of the house enjoying the fresh summer breeze and a DQ treat. It's not easy running this family business of ours, especially when you're juggling so many priorities. We do it because it keeps us closer to our family. And we love it because it's a good product with a nice and friendly environment. It's a product that we feel great about.

Love your job. Years ago, I used to think that you could have a high income and that would be the sole requirement for a satisfying job. Today, I don't believe that. My sisters and I make absolutely nothing from our parents' Dairy Queen business and we still love it.

This is about passion. It's about getting up in the morning for the purpose of adding value to something. Fitting into something and knowing that you'll be missed if you don't show. To be successful in a business, you must find the work that you're doing interesting, exciting, challenging, or just plain old fun. It must engage you and make you want to do it better. You may not be selling banana splits, but you're selling something to a customer who needs that product or service. And if you want to do it well, you have to believe in that product or service. In your eyes, your product or service may not match the appeal of a DQ treat, but in the customer's perspective it just might be the treat he or she needs. Gotta love your soft serve!

# 18

# Always Offer Your Delivery Guys a Milk Shake

Our family has a lot of unwritten rules that have been instilled in me from childhood. One of these is that any person who comes into our home is offered a glass of water, juice, or soda. Be it a neighbor, the newspaper boy collecting his money, or the sofa delivery guys. My sisters and I have always abided by this simple rule.

Almost naturally, this bit of etiquette extends to the people we work with in our store—especially our delivery guys, who come in about twice a week. These guys really work hard—especially in the summer heat. They carry heavy bags of milk, boxes, tubs of ice cream, and more. Sometimes we're too busy with work to have much time to chat when they come to drop off the inventory order, but we do try to make time to get to know them a little better and *always* ask them if they'd like something cold to drink, like a milk shake. On a hot summer day, most of them take us up on that milk shake and are very appreciative. My parents have built a personal relationship with these guys over the years. They're not just our delivery guys—they're our friends. It comes naturally for my parents to treat them in this manner.

More than a dozen times, this professional kindness has helped us to weather many storms known as inventory shortages. Running out of a specific ice cream before a holiday weekend is a nightmare, and usually the supplier doesn't send out another delivery truck because the drivers are off those days. But if the supplier finds a driver willing to do it, they

OK it. Our delivery guys have gone out of their way for us because they know how important it is to our business. They've come through because we've treated them well—like more than just inventory suppliers; like friends.

Treat your delivery guys or suppliers nicely because it is the right thing to do and good for your business. Having a respectful and kind relationship with them makes your job easier and ensures smooth operations for your business. Anything is possible when you have a good relationship with your suppliers.

## 19

# Bring Them in on a Saturday Morning

Our second year into the Dairy Queen business, we were faced with a big problem. We had retained just one employee from the previous year. We hired six new workers, but they still had to go through training and summer was quickly approaching. Our usual training method was about managing customers "on the job," meaning that when the employee came in, he would start serving customers with Mom and learn how to make everything the customer had ordered on the spot. This was a slow process because each customer ordered a different treat and so the employee got a chance to make each item (for example, a hot fudge sundae) only once or twice during the day. Serving hundreds of customers over the course of a month ensured they would learn how to make everything on our menu. But we had six new employees—almost our entire staff—who were working and training on different shifts. This meant that they weren't going to be ready for another four to five weeks at the earliest. It quickly became clear that our usual training method wasn't going to cut it. We needed fully trained people ready to go right away.

We usually open the store at 11:30 a.m. I proposed to my parents that we bring all the new hires in on Saturday morning at 9:00 a.m. and train them for two hours straight—without serving any customers. We would walk them through making everything from a cone to a sundae and also show them how to clean and how to serve customers.

They could ask questions and take notes at their own leisure without having to worry about being rushed because customers were waiting. "Why would they come in on a Saturday morning just to get trained?" asked my mom. "Because we would be paying them," I responded. "No way! I'm not paying them to come in and not serve any customers," was my mom's reply. It took me about two minutes to convince her and my dad that it was not only a good idea, but in fact our *only* option if we wanted to get our employees ready quickly. We did it. All of them came for two hours every Saturday for three weeks. With that training period as well as "on the job" training, they were ready!

Your employees represent you, your company, and your products and services. Make sure you invest in them. Whether it's the weekend or a Wednesday—train them. Take time out of your schedule to spend an hour talking to them about what they're doing and offer them encouragement and guidance on how to do it better. As managers and businesspeople, we have to recognize that our job is mainly about helping our employees do the right things so that we make it easier for our business to succeed.

If you believe that your employees are an important asset to your business, then show them by investing in their training. This doesn't have to be a Harvard executive education-training program. It can be as simple as taking time out of a normal day to talk to them. Take them out for coffee in the middle of the afternoon. Ask them to come in earlier in the morning to share a pastry. Do something that provides them with training or coaching in an environment that is not rushed. This investment will give you and your business a tremendous return and have them better prepared for managing those customers regardless of the season.

# 2 0

# Take Good Care
# of Your Machines

Ice cream machines are huge, expensive, and a real pain in the neck when they don't work. Somehow they always give us trouble during a hot summer day when there are twenty people waiting in line. The previous owner trained us on how to maintain the machines but didn't tell us that they were going to go on the blink on occasion and during the worst times. The typical new soft serve ice cream machine is bulky, energy draining, and can cost anywhere from $10,000 to $30,000. These machines last about twenty years in some cases but do require regular maintenance to keep them going.

We learned this lesson the hard way one summer when our soft serve vanilla machine broke down. Soft serve vanilla is our most popular ice cream because it is used in making everything from banana splits to cones and sundaes. At about 2:00 p.m., our machine started to make some funny noises. Soon it just stopped pumping out ice cream altogether. Most Sundays are hot and busy thanks to the lively after-church crowd, and this Sunday was no exception. Of course everyone wanted soft vanilla and we had to tell them they could only have hard vanilla ice cream because the machine was broken. We lost a few customers that day but managed to nicely persuade most of them to get an equally delicious alternate flavor.

By the next day, we had gotten the machine fixed and were back in action. But the fact that we lost customers the previous day simply because we did not do a good job of maintaining the machine when it *wasn't* giving us trouble was unacceptable. According to the expert who fixed our machine, all we needed to do to avoid this incident was to lubricate some of the parts in the machine every couple of weeks. Our lack of proactive maintenance led to our losing customers and also took away from our credibility as a consistent supplier of ice cream treats. Some customers took our broken machine in stride. But for others, they were counting on us to provide them with the products we're known for and we let them down.

To operate successfully, every business depends on some type of equipment, whether it's a computer network, a highly sophisticated manufacturing facility, or a cash register. This equipment is essential to the business and should be maintained at all costs. Losing customers because of failed equipment is a disaster that can, in most cases, be avoided. Take good care of your machines and they'll take good care of your business.

## 21

# Check the Weather
# Before You Order

As with most businesses, our Dairy Queen store has its slow times. Early on, my parents decided to put in a television to keep them entertained as they went about cleaning and refilling the stock when there were no customers to wait on. But ever since, one of our family rituals is to watch the weather forecast on the five o'clock news. Knowing what the weather will be like during the week enables us to plan our inventory accordingly. If it's going to be sunny and eighty degrees all week, we know to order more ice cream and milk, because a hot week means a busy week. If we order too much milk for Monday and it rains the next five days straight, we end up wasting a lot of money because we have to throw out the milk that might have gone bad. Also, ordering too much inventory ties up our cash flow when we might need it for something else.

While the weather forecast may not be crucial to your business, environmental trends can have a significant impact. Political, economic, and consumer preferences are three important environmental elements that one needs to look at when planning for the future of the business. Consumer preferences don't necessarily shift overnight. What we've observed is that they shift slowly, with the younger generation leading the way.

Of course no one can predict the future but there are some things that signal what the "weather" is going to be like. The lesson here is one of keeping an eye on the environment and planning accordingly. Look at the trends and see where your customer and business are headed. Look around to see if you're going in the right direction or if something is brewing that may threaten your business model. And then do something about it. If you think that the economy is going to be in trouble, then don't invest in expanding.

The weather is symbolic of trends in the environment. And like a set of storm clouds, trends can move into your business over a short period of time and bring a lot of rain. The trick is not to fight change. Identify the trend, figure out the impact on your business, develop a plan, and then make the appropriate changes to your business. The last thing you want is to have a lot of "ice cream" on hand when it's pouring rain outside.

# 22

# Pay Your Bills
# on Time

**W**hile I was in college and taking some accounting classes, my parents entrusted me with the task of taking care of the bills at the store. Boy, I sure got myself into something I wasn't ready for. That accounting class did not prepare me for making the payroll, calling in the inventory, paying the bills, making the deposits, and everything else. For a few months, I inadvertently got late on payments to the "sprinkles" guy. This small company sold us deliciously crunchy rainbow- and chocolate-colored sprinkles that went on cones and sundaes. I must have put their invoices in a folder and simply forgotten about them.

That mistake caused us some problems for a while. Before they informed us of the delay in payments, they started throwing subtle hints at us. While placing orders over the phone, we would be put on hold for a very long time; our deliveries would show up late; and the customer service person I often spoke with started becoming more and more curt with me. It was unbelievable. It wasn't until we got a very firm collection notice one day that I realized I made a mistake somewhere. Right away, I called the owner of the business and apologized for not paying the bills on time. It was an honest mistake and he realized it when he received the check in the mail a few days later. I don't think he actually believed it had been an honest mistake until he cashed the check. He did call me the following week and said he was a little surprised that this whole thing happened because he knew we had been such good customers up until that time. He went on to explain that he was embarrassed for the way he and his staff had treated us and that it was not their usual behavior. Apparently, any customers who didn't pay their bills were given this kind of "cold shoulder" treatment.

I had never before experienced the cold shoulder from suppliers and so I inquired about it from a supplier I was on friendly terms with—Joe, the hard ice cream delivery guy. Joe sat me down and explained the importance of paying our bills on time. According to Joe, the relationship between companies and their suppliers was about respect. By not making paying the bills on time a priority, companies would get a bad reputation among the suppliers. The suppliers would react by not giving them good customer service or a fast response to their orders if the company didn't have enough respect to pay the supplier on time.

Seems pretty simple, right? But it's a lesson I had to learn the hard way. In business there is always a give-and-take. Sometimes you're on the giving end and sometimes on the receiving end. If you expect your customers to pay you for your hard work, then you should have the common decency to pay your suppliers for *their* hard work. They count on that income just as much as you count on the income from your customers. A good relationship between you and your suppliers is invaluable for your business in terms of better customer service, more favorable finance terms, or just plain faster deliveries. For obvious reasons, a customer who pays on time is valued. And a valued customer can demand many favorable terms—which include not paying during the tough times. In fact, one of our suppliers offered a payment plan where we didn't have to pay him during the winter months when we are short of cash flow and pay him with no interest during the summer. He recognized our situation and considering our solid payment history offered us a good deal.

Since that incident, we've never neglected to pay our bills on time and have benefited greatly in terms of better discounts and faster and more frequent delivery times. Always pay your bills on time. It's the fair thing to do and can lead to enormous rewards for your business in the long run.

## 23

# Go a Mile for Cheaper Milk

**M**y dad is very detail-oriented. He questions just about *everything*. Growing up, this used to annoy the heck out of me. He does the same with the business, especially when it comes to supply costs. One of his favorite things is saving money the old-fashioned way—being frugal.

We get most of our milk supplies from the dairy that is subcontracted by DQ headquarters, but on occasion we have to get a couple of gallons of milk from the local supermarket. When we first started to do this, we would get the milk from the big supermarket on the way to our Dairy Queen store. But over time, my dad found the cheapest place to buy milk was a small grocery store located a bit farther away. About twice a week, my dad gets in the car and drives down to that little grocery store to buy milk. He does this even though there's a small convenience store right next door to our Dairy Queen! Sure, the milk next door is more expensive, but to me the convenience of it is worth paying the extra few cents. Whenever I would work on the weekends, I would go next door and buy the milk. Although it wasn't such a big deal to me, my dad wasn't too happy about it.

For some people it might not make sense to save a few cents at the expense of your time and the extra gas mileage, but to my dad it made a difference. And he always made sure to pick up the milk when he was already driving by the store for another reason. Over the years, I noticed that he and my mom carried this frugal habit into other things: They squeeze the last amount of soap from the bottle by putting in a little bit of water or pitch in with other Dairy Queens to buy certain products or services in bulk. My sisters and I never really paid much attention to these details while we were growing up, mostly because saving a buck or two here and there wasn't something we thought about when we were young. We just wanted convenience. But over time, it does add up.

It is not necessarily the few cents we would save that is the point of this lesson—it is the frame of mind that leads one to behave in such a way. Frugality is one of those things that some people are born with and others, like myself, are not. In the last few years, I've learned to be more frugal simply because it just doesn't make sense to waste money when you don't have to!

Encourage frugality. Shop around and look long and hard and find ways where you can save money in your business. It might mean not buying something that is "nice to have" or it might just mean finding good deals. Having a consistently frugal frame of mind will help you lower your costs and thus boost your profit. Going that extra mile for your "cheaper milk" may make the difference in sustaining a successful business.

# 24

# Befriend a Neighbor with a Freezer

One summer afternoon, we'd been dutifully watching the weather forecast and heard that thunderstorms were expected for later that day. Not long after, dark clouds rolled in, and the rain began pouring down in earnest. It had been oppressively humid for weeks, so we looked forward to having a little rain. But it also meant a lull in business. But suddenly lightning started shooting sporadically across the sky. The next thing we knew, the power went out.

After a few minutes, I started getting worried. I knew what a power outage meant for the ice cream. Half an hour later, the lights were still out. Some of the ice cream started melting and I had to take action. I spoke to the power company, and found out that the power outage was concentrated in a two-mile radius around our area. This meant that some of the other places in town had power. I called a few of the other restaurants in the neighborhood, but couldn't find anyplace that had the kind of freezer we needed to keep the ice cream frozen. I had never really paid attention to the places in the neighborhood, so finding a place with a freezer took some time. Even though I had lived and worked in the area for years, I actually had to look in the yellow pages to find a place that might have the kind of freezer we needed!

Having located a restaurant that would serve our needs, I called and introduced myself to the manager and asked if we could use their cooler to store some of our products until our power came back on. I was a complete stranger to him and he didn't really know how to react. He asked how long I would need it and what I would be storing. After assuring him that we would not take up a lot of space or disturb his business, I loaded up my car with as many products as I could and headed over to the restaurant.

We stored only a few things in his small refrigerator, given that he didn't have much space. The power came back on a couple of hours later and though a few products had to be thrown out, we didn't really have such a drastic meltdown.

Get to know your neighbors. Regardless of whether they are your competitors, stop by and introduce yourself. Give them a free sundae or simply a good morning once in a while. They may teach you something or share some valuable insight about the community. During the opening of our new DQ store, the first thing my parents did was introduce themselves to the local shops in the area. At the very least, you may have a nice conversation with a fellow store owner. And if your lights go out, you will now have a friend to call and ask for help.

# 25

# Know the
# Fat Content

Over the last fifteen years, more people have become concerned about calories, fat, and carbohydrate content than ever before. Although calorie-conscious consumers were frequently in the store during the frozen yogurt craze in the mid-'90s, I don't think they were as extreme as they are today. I generally believe that when treating themselves to a sweet treat, most people don't bother with counting calories. Initially, I never really bothered to look at the labels of our products. But sure enough, customers started asking about calorie content, and not knowing the details of our product left me embarrassed a few times.

Some might think that it isn't that important to inform a customer how many calories are in a cone. What's the big deal? It's usually "a lot" anyway. But it is important information to the consumer. People who are watching their diet or living with diabetes and watching their sugar intake need to know basic data about what they are consuming. You have to respect that and account for it. Providing accurate answers to customers' questions defines your credibility to a large extent. It is important for us to get this right with customers because in the absence of accurate information, they may perceive the content to be worse than it actually is, which could lead them to come into the store less frequently.

Know as much in-depth information as you can about all aspects of your product. Know it as if your business depended on it. Ask questions, talk to people, read—dig deeper. This applies not only to knowledge about your product but also about your finances, employee relationships, supplier management, and more. Knowledge can arm you with the confidence you will need to make important decisions. One way of garnering this information is to ask lots of questions about everything. Demonstrate your curiosity to your employees, colleagues, and team in a genuine way. Knowing the details will only add to the richness of your capability, and in turn help you provide great customer service while saving you some embarrassing moments.

# 26

# Show Them
# How to Serve

On a Friday evening around 7:00 p.m., I arrived at the store exhausted. I had just come from a weeklong business trip abroad for my "real" job. After being in three countries in five days, the last thing I wanted to do was to help out at the store. But given that it was eighty-five degrees out and both my sisters were out of town, I knew my mom had been working all day and had to be pretty tired. As I've done many times before, I went into the store and sent her home to take a break, despite her objections. We started getting busy about an hour later and served customers nonstop until about 11:30 p.m. Neither the employees nor the customers knew that earlier that day I had worked on complex business issues with colleagues in three other countries and had literally just gotten off the plane in Newark. While I was helping one of the employees with the messy garbage in the parking lot, he asked me about what I did earlier in the week and I told him of my business trip. After six years in this type of role in my corporate job, these trips were so commonplace for me that I didn't really see it as a big deal. But our DQ employees thought it was "just so cool" to do that.

There were three employees working that night who were relatively new to the store. All of them had just started working with us only a couple of weeks earlier. During the course of the night we served customers, cleaned the spills, and made cakes. Somewhere in the conversation they asked

me why I was up in the front line serving those customers when I could have stayed in the back and
just relaxed a bit. Without thinking, I answered that
I didn't think serving customers was actually
"working." I was tired from the long journey but I
did what I had to do—relieve Mom at the store and
serve those customers. What's the big deal? I
thought. Those kids ended up staying with us for a
few summers—which is longer than most since they
don't normally come back after going away to college. Over those summers they saw my sisters and
me do the same thing—work in our professional
jobs during the week and still come in each weekend to help out. And while we "helped out," we
didn't just sit there in the back of the store and
watch TV, which we could have done easily. We
worked the front lines, took out the garbage, and
did everything else that our employees do. Many
years later some of our employees dropped by the
store, after having graduated from college and
started jobs. Across the board, all of them talked

very positively of their experience working at the store during their formative teenage years, and told us they had been especially inspired by our work ethic.

I'm not sure if it is our work ethic that distinguishes my family—I would simply call it our leadership. Even during our training period, we educate our new and impressionable employees on proper ways to serve customers by showing them how it's done. In their first two days, we stand side by side with them when they serve customers. We do the talking on the first day and work with them to make the products, especially the cones with the special DQ curl on top. On the second day, we stand next to them but let them take the lead and interact with the customer directly while still helping them to make products correctly. We encourage them to use simple language during interactions and always smile along with them.

The word "leadership" is often thrown around

in place of "management" or when we want to praise someone for doing something unexpectedly. Our experience with leadership is a little different. For our business, it's about doing right by our people. It's about the way we interact with them, coach them, work with them, and nurture them to become leaders on their own. More importantly, leadership is about working with them up in the front line serving customers. When we train our employees, we try to guide them in the direction of being self-aware businesspeople who should take action on their own. And just because we're done training them doesn't mean that we sit back and watch TV in the back. We work the front lines—observing, helping, guiding, and being a model for the type of behavior we want to see in our own employees.

Leadership is less about knowing the right thing to do and more about helping your staff achieve success. We do it by working side by side with our people, modeling the behavior so that they learn and grow. It's not about making a perfect-sized soft serve cone. It is about helping your employees, colleagues, and team achieve success. We do this in a number of ways, but the primary way is by showing them how it's done and then getting out of the way as they master it themselves.

## 27

# Close the Store on Time

In the early years, we were really hungry for customers. We wanted the business to succeed and were willing to do anything to get new customers and keep them. We were so eager that we would stay open until 12:30 a.m. or 1:00 a.m. when were supposed to close at 11:00 p.m. By the time we got home it would be two in the morning! We did this for a few summers. Customers coming from a late movie would start lining up at our store around midnight wanting a late-night treat.

Staying open so late at night wasn't such a big deal at the time because we made good money and kept those late-night customers happy. But after a while it got to us. Closing at 1:00 a.m. and then coming back to open the store again at 11:00 a.m. was physically draining. We weren't as productive during the course of the day, either. Those extra few dollars earned at midnight just weren't worth it when we looked at what it did to our health and well-being. So we just stopped.

Now we close our doors at 11:00 p.m. The only exceptions are if there's a huge line of people waiting or the occasional husband with a pregnant wife in the car. By forcing ourselves to close on time, we have also conditioned our customers to show up before our 11:00 p.m. closing.

Work will never end. You can literally stay "in the store" all night long. Go home at a decent time, spend time with your family, and get good rest. No amount of work is worth losing precious time with your family or harming your health. By closing your store on time, you'll have greater satisfaction in your personal life, be better prepared to go to work the next day, and have a higher level of enthusiasm about the job.

## 28

# Don't Let the Mr. Misty Go to Your Head

My wife, my sisters, and I all have jobs that would be considered "professional" by most people. My sisters are both business school graduates who work for Fortune 500 companies. My wife is a practicing optometrist. As for myself, I have both undergraduate and graduate degrees in marketing and international business and have worked for the last thirteen years at one of the largest companies in the world. From traveling to different countries to mopping the floors, we've had a wide variety of on-the-job experiences. All of us have seen and done a lot. So when a teenager I'm serving a sundae to tells me that I'm stupid for getting his ice cream flavor wrong, it's bound to raise my ire. I start to think, How can this kid tell me I'm stupid? I've done and seen more things in a year than this kid has done in his lifetime.

Sometimes your ego wants to take control and tell the rude customer that you're better than he is. But then you realize that you really don't know anything about him and that by making assumptions about someone you don't even know you are reducing yourself to his bad manners. It's hard to hold back responding to some of these rude customers, but attacking them is bad for business and for your self-respect. All in all, it's really not the right thing to do.

If I respond in kind to a rude customer, he'll probably never come back. And if we did that all the time, we wouldn't have many customers. I see more

and more people with sour faces in the la.. .. ,
and I think about all the troubles they may be going
through in their lives. Whenever my wife or my sisters tell me that they've had a rude customer or col-
league, I tell them to let it go. You can never know
what problems the person may be going through.
Maybe they or someone in their family has a serious
illness or they're unhappy about their job. Maybe
they are simply having a bad day.

You have to show humility and professionalism
in the face of rudeness. The moment you give attitude back, you can expect your customer to notice
it and not come to your store again. Who would
want to come to a place where the employees intim-
idate and embarrass them? Not me. And probably
not any customer who has a choice—he'd rather go
to your competition!

Dealing with a rude customer is a lot like drink-
ing a Mr. Misty too fast—both can give you a
headache! Likewise when we tend to make fast
judgments about people, which we end up paying

for later. Don't let the Mr. Misty go to your head too quickly—don't rush to judge, and be humble. At the end of the day, all you want is to be able to sell your products and services and go home. By controlling your ego and being humble, you're doing the right thing for your peace of mind and your business.

# 29

# Go to the
# Convention

Every two years, International Dairy Queen holds a convention for its franchises across the world. During the early years, we were never "convention" people but couldn't pass up the one that International Dairy Queen had in Hawaii. One December, we took the plunge and went off to Honolulu for the convention. We met lots of hardworking families just like us from across the United States. It was incredible to meet people who related to us on so many levels. We had so many experiences in common, from having to deal with family issues in the business to buying the right kind of hot fudge. We met our national suppliers, the marketing people from Dairy Queen Headquarters, as well as the president of International Dairy Queen.

One of the families we met was from Wyoming. The couple was in their late fifties and had a young daughter and son, about eighteen and sixteen respectively. Not only did they buy their store around the same time we bought ours, but also their family dynamics were similar to ours. Their kids didn't "love" working at the store any more than we did at the time. We went to dinner together and shared some great stories. They even showed us a few tricks of the trade that we didn't know about.

Coming back from this trip, I realized that we weren't alone. Other people just like us from across the country were going through the same wonderful and challenging times in running a Dairy Queen franchise. Knowing that our challenges were uni-

# 3 0

# Sponsor a Little League Team

**S**ponsoring that Little League baseball team was probably one of the coolest things we've ever done. We got involved because one of our regular customers was a coach for a local Little League team. It was a bit expensive, but we did it because he had been a good customer and it seemed like the right thing to do at the time.

By being actively engaged in our community, we made a difference to this Little League team. By sponsoring them and giving them free ice cream on occasion, we were doing our part in being active members of our community. Sure we benefited when buses of kids showed up at the store after a game with their parents and siblings, but more importantly we learned that a business owes something to the community in which it operates. Customers in the neighborhood provide us with the income to operate, and so the least we can do is give something back. Give something back to the community in which you work or live. A business has a life of its own and so should be actively engaged in the community in which it operates. It's a give-and-take. You can't just expect to take and not give something. Whether it's volunteering at a community center or a hospital, being a Big Brother or Sister, or simply sponsoring a Little League team—get involved and give something back. You'll be doing a good service to those who bring in the income for your business.

# Conclusion

**W**orking at my family's Dairy Queen business has taught me many valuable lessons. The most important lesson is that the behaviors required for success in business are the same as those needed for success in life: engaging fully in everything you do, having and following some core principles or truths, and being fair and kind to all people. At the end of the day, it is not about how many cones I serve or my title and responsibility in a Fortune 500 company. It's about the value I bring to others—family, friends, colleagues, employees, and customers.

On a day-to-day basis, that value is the product or service we provide our customers.

In our Dairy Queen, we don't sell a product—we sell an emotional experience. We're selling the positive feeling and experience associated with a visit to our store. What a wonderful feeling it is to see a child's eyes light up as she sees that ice cream cone headed toward her. Or to make the perfect hot fudge sundae for a lady who's had a tough day at work. Pleasing our customers by creating that experience is what makes it worthwhile for me, and successful for the business. And although you may not be serving ice cream cones, each day you do have the same opportunity to benefit your business by Treating Your Customers!

*"Sometimes it is the simplest things that provide life's greatest lessons."*

# Treat Your Customers Cheat Sheet

| THE STORY | THE BUSINESS LESSON |
| --- | --- |
| 1. They're not just customers— they're people | Everyone's human |
| 2. Know their names and their favorite flavor | Know your customers |
| 3. The customer is still royalty | Treat them like gold |
| 4. Don't make them wait | Be attentive |
| 5. Once in a while, taste your own ice cream | Know what you're selling |
| 6. If they ask for a medium cone—give them a medium cone | Provide consistency |
| 7. Don't serve rotten bananas | Give quality |

| | |
|---|---|
| 8. Never forget the plain old vanilla | Cash cow |
| 9. Always replace a dropped cone | Integrity is priceless |
| 10. Want whipped cream and nuts on that? | Up-sell |
| 11. The cherry is always free | Touch the customer emotionally |
| 12. Greet them and leave them with a smile | Positive first contact is crucial |
| 13. The boss is not the customer | Focus on what's really important |
| 14. Become a cake expert | Embrace new skills/ technology |
| 15. Don't raise prices if Mom feels guilty | Do the right thing |
| 16. When it's time to lean, it's time to clean | Encourage action |
| 17. Gotta love your soft serve | Love what you do |
| 18. Always offer your delivery guys a milk shake | Suppliers are invaluable |
| 19. Bring them in on a Saturday morning | Invest in your people |

20. Take good care of your machines — Update your equipment

21. Check the weather before you order — Plan accordingly

22. Pay your bills on time — Good credit—good terms

23. Go a mile for cheaper milk — Frugality should be a habit

24. Befriend a neighbor with a freezer — Know everybody around you

25. Know the fat content — Details, details, details

26. Show them how to serve — Lead by example

27. Close the store on time — Have a life outside of work

28. Don't let the Mr. Misty go to your head — Be humble

29. Go to the convention — Learn from others

30. Sponsor a Little League team — Be a part of your community

**Bob Miglani** has been working in a Fortune 500 Company for the last thirteen years, where he has had positions of increasing responsibility leading into his current role as Senior Director of Public Affairs. A well-respected leader in his field, he has been at the forefront of identifying and embracing new and emerging customers and developing innovative partnerships. He continues to serve a different type of customer in his spare time on the weekends and some holidays at his family's Dairy Queen® restaurant, which he has helped manage for over twenty years.